# Kids in Ancient Egypt

The Rosen Publishing Group's
**PowerKids Press**™
New York

Published in 1999 by The Rosen Publishing Group, Inc.
29 East 21st Street, New York, NY 10010

First Edition

Book Design: Danielle Primiceri

Photo Credits: Cover and p. 16 © Trip / Viesti Collection, Inc.; pp. 8, 12, 20 © Corbis-Bettman; p. 4 © Gamma Liaison International; p. 7 © Graphic House / Corbis-Bettman; p. 11 © Joe Viesti / Viesti Associates, Inc.; p. 15 © Erich Lessing; p. 19 © Art Resource.

Wroble, Lisa A.
     Kids in ancient Egypt / by Lisa A. Wroble.
          p.    cm.—(Kids throughout history)
     Includes index.
     Summary: Describes the daily life of children in ancient Egypt, including housing, clothes, food, and religion.
     ISBN 0-8239-5256-8
     1. Egypt—Social life and customs—To 332 B.C.—Juvenile literature. 2. Children—Egypt—Juvenile literature. [1. Egypt—Civilization.] I. Title. II. Series: Wroble, Lisa A. Kids throughout history.
     DT61.W77 1998
     305.23'0932—dc21                                                                          97-49581
                                                                                                      CIP
                                                                                                       AC

Manufactured in the United States of America

# Contents

# Ancient Egypt

Egypt is a country in northern Africa. Ancient Egypt was one of the first **civilizations** (SIH-vih-lih-ZAY-shunz) in history. It lasted from about 3100 BC to 640 AD. A **pharaoh** (FAYR-oh) ruled all of Egypt. In honor of each pharaoh, Egyptians built **statues** (STA-chooz) and giant **tombs** (TOOMZ) called **pyramids** (PEER-uh-midz) that are still standing today. Life in ancient Egypt centered around the Nile River. The Egyptians used the Nile as a kind of water highway to carry goods for trade to other civilizations.

◀ *The Great Sphinx, seen here, has the head of a pharaoh and the body of a lion.*

# Gift of the Nile

Ancient Egypt was called the gift of the Nile. The Nile gave Egyptians drinking water, a place to fish, water for their crops, and plenty of animals living at its edges for people to hunt. Every June, the Nile flooded. Months later, the waters went down, leaving behind rich black soil. Farmers then planted their crops in this soil. Large boats carried goods, such as glass, to other cities. Often the boats brought back gold and ivory as well as the large stone blocks that were used to build the pyramids.

*Without the Nile River, ancient Egyptians may not have survived to build their great civilization.* ▶

# An Egyptian City

**S**hen was a nine-year-old boy. He lived in Memphis, the capital of ancient Egypt, located at the top of the Nile. The pharaoh's palace and a temple were at the center of the city. Craftspeople, who sold goods such as cloth, tools, bricks, and jewelry, built their shops around the palace. The people of Memphis also made their homes here. Farmers, like Shen's father, lived on the edge of the city. They needed a lot of land to grow their crops and raise farm animals.

*Temples, such as the great Temple of Luxor, could be found in most cities and were an important part of daily life in ancient Egypt.*

# Shen's House

Shen's house was built of bricks that were made from sun-baked mud. Dirt floors were covered with mats. Small windows helped keep the house cool. Stairs led from the living area up to a flat roof. Many Egyptian families held parties on their rooftops. And on very hot nights Shen would even sleep up there! Shen's mother cooked the family meals outside in the **courtyard** (KORT-yard). There she kept large jars and big baskets that stored grains and food for their animals.

*Families in ancient Egypt lived in homes much like those found in modern-day Egypt.* ▶

# Clothes

The weather in ancient Egypt was very hot. So Egyptians wore clothes made of thin **linen** (LIN-en) to help keep cool. Men wore knee-length linen **kilts** (KILTZ), which looked like skirts. Shen also wore a kilt, but he wrapped it between his legs and around his waist as other young boys did. Shen's mother and his sister wore long linen dresses. Sometimes they braided their hair. Like many boys in ancient Egypt, Shen's head was shaved except for one lock of hair on the side of his head.

◄ *Ancient Egyptians dressed in plain clothes, but both men and women wore beautiful jewelry.*

# Food

Shen's mother often ground grain into flour to make bread. This was Shen's favorite food. Shen fished in the Nile. And he hunted ducks and geese with his father. Shen's mother used a clay oven and an open fire in the courtyard to cook the meat they brought home. She also served cheese, beans, garlic, and onions with the meat. Ancient Egyptians ate dessert too. Fruits, such as figs and grapes, were a delicious treat. And for special parties, Shen's mother even baked fancy cakes in the shapes of animals.

*In ancient Egypt, the whole family often went on hunting trips together.* ▶

# Religion

Ancient Egyptians believed that beings greater than humans called gods and goddesses controlled everything in their lives. Egyptians also thought their spirits would live with these gods after death. Tombs were made, often in the pyramids, to hold the **mummies** (MUM-eez) of the pharaohs. Food and jewels were placed in the tombs for use in the **afterlife** (AF-ter-LYF). But thieves knew of the riches in these tombs and often stole them. So Egyptians began to hide the tombs underground. Fake tunnels and rooms were made to fool robbers.

◄ *Colorful scenes found on the walls of a tomb were thought to protect the mummy's spirit.*

# Learning and Playing

Most girls did not go to school. Instead, they learned to weave and cook from their mothers. Boys went to school only if they were to become **scribes** (SKRYBZ) or priests. They learned to read and write **hieroglyphics** (HY-er-uh-GLIF-iks). Math and **geography** (jee-AH-gruh-fee) were also taught. Kids found time to have fun too. They played with dolls, tops, balls, and toys with parts that moved. They also had pets, such as cats, monkeys, and birds. Board games, such as **senet** (SEN-it), and music were also popular.

*The Rosetta stone contains three ancient forms of writing, including hieroglyphics. Its discovery helped people understand Egyptian writing.* ▶

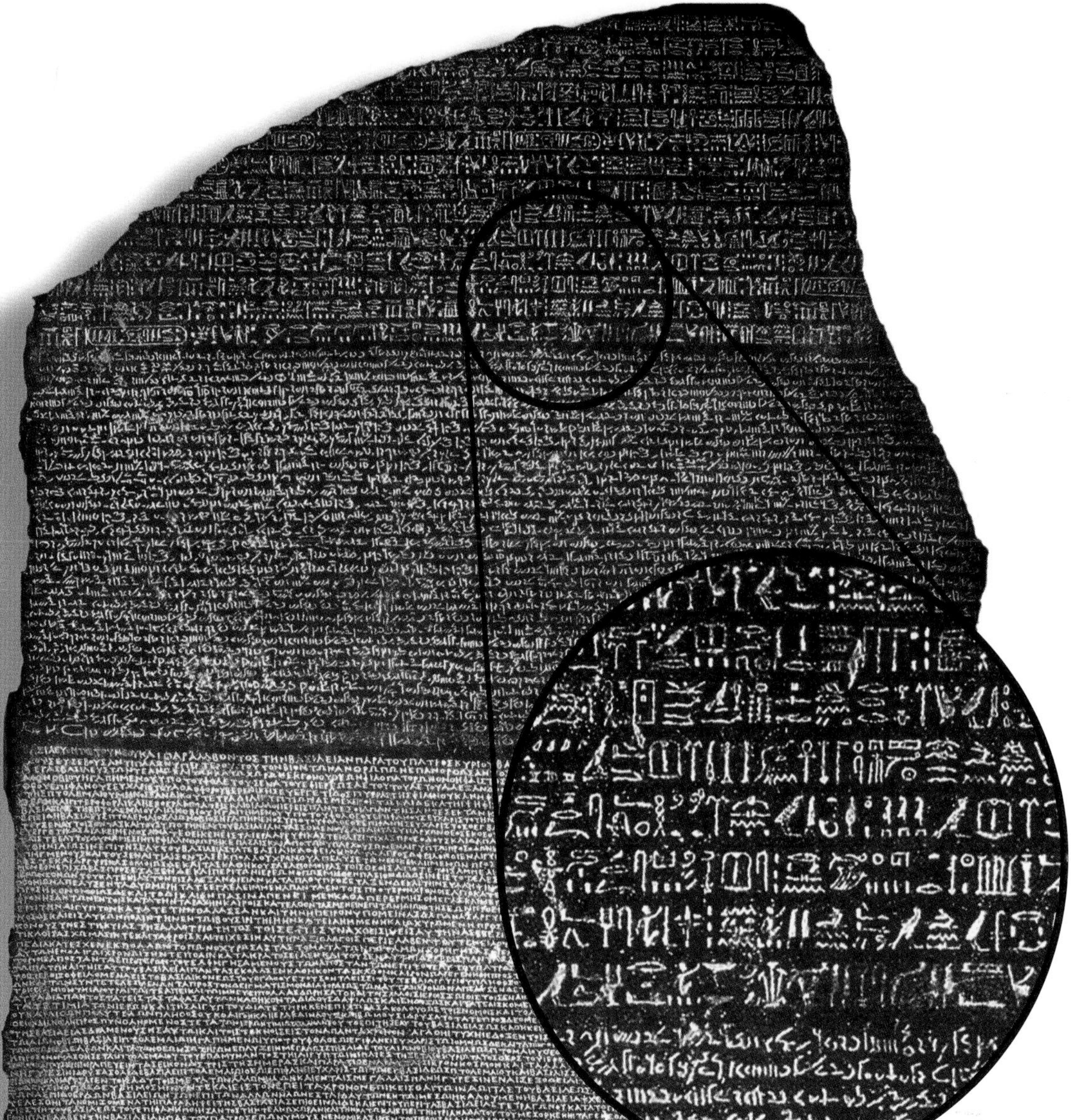

# Work

Farmers, like Shen's father, used animals to push seeds into the ground when they planted crops. From those seeds grew grapes, figs, and dates. Some of these crops would be sent to the pharaoh's palace. Shen's father also traded some fruit for other farmers' crops so his family could enjoy many different foods. While the Nile was flooded, farmers could not farm. So the pharaohs would order them to help build the pyramids. The largest Egyptian pyramid took more than 20,000 men over twenty years to build.

◀ *In addition to farmers, skilled laborers were hired to help build the pyramids. They were paid with food and supplies needed for daily living.*

# Improving Life

The people of ancient Egypt discovered many things that made their lives and our lives better. Using fibers from the **papyrus** (puh-PY-ris) plant, they made long sheets of paper on which they wrote. These were rolled into **scrolls** (SKROHLZ). A great library was built in the ancient city of Alexandria to store these scrolls. Ancient Egyptians also learned how to measure distance and weight. And, by watching where the stars were in the sky each time the Nile flooded, they created a 365-day calendar that we still use today.

# Glossary

**afterlife** (AF-ter-LYF) Another life or world that people believe they will go to after they die.

**civilization** (SIH-vih-lih-ZAY-shun) A group of people living in an organized and similar way.

**courtyard** (KORT-yard) An open space enclosed by walls that is in or near a building.

**geography** (jee-AH-gruh-fee) The study of the earth's surface.

**hieroglyphics** (HY-er-uh-GLIF-iks) A form of writing that uses over 700 pictures for different words and sounds.

**kilt** (KILT) A cloth wrapped around the waist and tied or pinned.

**linen** (LIN-en) A fine cloth made from the fibers of a plant.

**mummy** (MUM-ee) A body carefully prepared for burial.

**papyrus** (puh-PY-ris) A tall water plant that is peeled and pounded into paper-like sheets.

**pharaoh** (FAYR-oh) An ancient Egyptian ruler.

**pyramid** (PEER-uh-mid) A large stone structure with a square bottom and triangular sides that meet at a point on top.

**scribe** (SKRYB) A person whose job is to copy books by hand.

**scroll** (SKROHL) A roll of paper used for writing.

**senet** (SEN-it) A board game played by ancient Egyptians.

**statue** (STA-choo) A carved image.

**tomb** (TOOM) A grave for someone who has died.

23

# Index